Public Mental Health

A Changing System in an Era of Managed Care

Public Mental Health

A Changing System in an Era of Managed Care

American Psychiatric Association

Office of Economic Affairs and Practice Management

The findings, opinions, and conclusions of this report do not necessarily represent the views of the officers, trustees, or all members of the American Psychiatric Association.

Other monographs on managed care available from the APA Office of Economic Affairs and Practice Management:

The Psychiatrist's Managed Care Primer (Order #2450)
The Psychiatrist's Guide to Practice Management (Order #2451)
The Psychiatrist's Guide to Managed Care Contracting (Order #2454)
The Psychiatrist's Guide to Capitation and Risk-Based Contracting (Order #2453)
Public Mental Health: A Changing System in an Era of Managed Care (Order #2452)
American Psychiatric Association Capitation Handbook (Order #2277)

To order, please contact:

American Psychiatric Press, Inc.
1400 K Street, N.W.
Washington, DC 20005
www.appi.org
1-800-368-5777
fax: 202-789-2648
e-mail: order@appi.org

Copyright © 1997
American Psychiatric Association
ALL RIGHTS RESERVED
Manufactured in the United States
of America on acid-free paper
First Edition
00 99 98 97
4 3 2 1

American Psychiatric Association
1400 K Street, N.W.
Washington, DC 20005

Library of Congress Cataloging-in-Publication Data
Public mental health : a changing system in an era of managed care /
    by American Psychiatric Association Office of Economic Affairs and
    Practice Management. — 1st ed.
        p.   cm.
    Includes bibliographical references.
    ISBN 0-89042-452-7
    1. Managed mental health care—United States.   2. Mental health
services—United States—Finance.   3. Insurance, Mental health—
United States.   4. Poor—Mental health services—United States—
Finance.   I. American Psychiatric Association. Office of Economic
Affairs and Practice Management.
    [DNLM: 1. Mental Health Services—economics—United States.
2. Managed Care Programs—United States.   3. Medicare—United
States.   4. Health Services Accessibility—United States.   WM 30
P9754 1997]
RA790.6.P794   1997
362.2'04252'0973—dc21
DNLM/DLC
for Library of Congress   97-11029
                                                                      CIP

British Library Cataloguing in Publication Data
A CIP record is available from the British Library.

Table of Contents

Introduction

Public mental health systems are undergoing tremendous changes, particularly with the increasing penetration of managed care into this market. As a result, it is more important than ever for psychiatrists who work with patients treated in public facilities to have an understanding of the new systems. This monograph, one of a series of five, is designed to facilitate that understanding. In this volume, we describe the changes evolving in public systems, special considerations for patients in this sector, and implications for the role of psychiatrists.

The APA would like to express its appreciation to Open Minds for its assistance preparing this document, to Robert T.M. Phillips, M.D., Ph.D., for making this project a reality, and to the following consultant advisors for lending their expertise:

> Richard Fields, M.D.
> Altha Stewart, M.D.
> Nancy Winters, M.D.

I would also like to thank the staff of the Office of Economic Affairs and Practice Management for their countless hours coordinating the project, conducting research, and editing and drafting text to make these products as useful as possible:

> Mary Graham, Director
> Katherine Moore, Health Economist
> Sajini Thomas, Health Economist
> Carolyn Heier, Industry Analyst

Jesse Gately, Research Assistant
Donna Hagler, Administrative Assistant

I am pleased to add this monograph to the APA's array of products and I hope that it assists psychiatrists in coping with managed care's penetration of public psychiatry.

Melvin Sabshin, M.D.

Melvin Sabshin, M.D.
Medical Director

The Evolution of Public Mental Health in the United States

Historically, the role of the public mental health system in the United States has been as a "safety net" for the uninsured and underinsured. Evolving from the scattered efforts to house or "contain" mentally ill people in early American history to the complex array of services available today, the history of the public mental health system in the United States has largely been a history of hospitals. Beginning with the founding of the Pennsylvania Hospital in 1752 through the reform movement led by Dorothea Dix in 1841 (leading to the construction of 32 hospitals for the care of the indigent mentally ill) to the deinstitutionalization trends of the last two decades and the creation of the community mental health center system, the public mental health system has often provided the only source of care for uninsured and indigent patients.

The modern public mental health system can trace its roots to 1946, with the establishment of the National Institute for Mental Health (NIMH).[1] Through its efforts and the work of the Joint Commission on Mental Illness and Health, Congress created the community mental health center (CMHC) system by passing legislation in 1963 and 1965.[2] The original concept embodied by the Community Mental Health Centers Act of 1963 was the development of a comprehensive, integrated, and coordinated system of mental health care, provided in the least restrictive environment. It was the intent of Congress that

---

[1] Powell, C.K. & Straub, J.H. Medicare and Managed Care Manual. New York: Thompson Publishing Group, 1996, p. 990.
[2] Ibid, p. 990.

II

CMHCs would be self-sustaining, and the initial grants were intended as seed money.[3]

Driven largely by program and grant funding, the public mental health system, through the CMHC system, provided a core set of mandated services that included landmark programs for children and the elderly. Along with these core services, the CMHC system pioneered programs that provided alternatives to hospitalization, facilitated rapid and early care, and maintained patients in their natural environments as much as possible. CMHCs developed the process of case management that in large part forms the core of the practice of managed mental health programs today.

In 1965, the federal government also established two fee-for-service health benefit plans: Medicare for the elderly and disabled, and Medicaid for individuals and families with limited income. Medicare, established by Title XVIII of the Social Security Act, is a federally administered health plan for people age 65 and over, people disabled for Social Security purposes for two years, and some people with end-stage renal disease. Medicaid, also created by Congress as Title XIX of the Social Security Act, is a federal/state matching entitlement program for low-income individuals or those who meet other specific requirements. Whereas Medicare is a single uniform federal program, Medicaid is actually not one, but many separate programs managed by the 50 states, the District of Columbia, Puerto Rico, and the U.S. territories. Both Medicaid and Medicare have become significant payers of treatment services for individuals with mental illnesses.

At the same time that the public financing of health services was increasing, the private (employer-sponsored) health system was evolving. Prior to 1940, few Americans had health insurance coverage. During World War II, however, many soldiers and their families had health insurance coverage for the first time, courtesy of the U.S. military. After the war, in order to compete for employees, companies

---

[3] Ray, C.G. & Oss, M.E. "National Community Mental Healthcare Council," OPEN MINDS, 1993, Vol. 6, No. 12, p. 2.

began offering health benefits programs. The health benefit model offered by most companies relied on fee-for-service payment mechanisms, with minimal financial participation by patients. Patient contribution to these health care payments was often limited to little or no copayment.

In the 1970s and 1980s, the federal government passed landmark legislation which greatly changed the financing and delivery of health benefits. The HMO Act of 1973 was intended to reduce employer health costs by permitting health care practitioners to organize health maintenance organizations (HMOs) to compete with health insurance plans.[4] Then, in 1974, Congress passed the Employee Retirement Income Security Act (ERISA), which encouraged employers to self-insure health benefits, essentially giving them the ability to create their own employer-managed health benefit plans.[5]

Both ERISA and the HMO Act had a significant impact on the psychiatric field. The HMO Act essentially institutionalized a minimum level of mental health benefits by failing to require the same level of comprehensive coverage for psychiatric care as it did for all other physical illnesses and health care services. ERISA gave employers the ability to design health benefit plans with wide latitude in terms of coverage. Because ERISA is federal legislation, employer-sponsored health plans are exempt from the minimum benefit requirements and mental health parity regulations passed by state legislatures. This has led to great disparities between the medical and psychiatric services paid for by employer-sponsored health insurance plans. As more employer-sponsored health plans have limited or eliminated mental health care benefits from their plans, the cost of providing care to the uninsured has shifted to the public mental health system, where it has steadily increased.

A step toward resolving the parity issue was taken with legislation passed by both houses of Congress and signed by President Clinton in

---

[4] Oss, M.E. & Mackie, J.J. "Behavioral Health Finance: How Did We Get Here?" *OPEN MINDS*, 1995, Vol. 9, No. 7, pp. 4–5.
[5] Sipkoff, M. & Oss, M.E. "How to Avoid Strategic Planning Pitfalls," *OPEN MINDS*, 1995, Vol. 8, No. 11.

II

1996. The mental health parity rider is effective January 1, 1998. The
bill requires employer-sponsored plans that offer mental health benefits to have the same annual and lifetime limits as those of other
medical services. In addition, 11 states have passed or are proposing
mental health parity laws, to date.

Until very recently, funding for private and public benefit plans has
been quite separate, and private health plans have generally had very
limited mental health benefits. For this reason, the public mental
health system has been the primary services provider for the poor, the
elderly, and the seriously mentally ill.

These traditional distinctions have begun to blur however. By the
1980s, the financing for the public mental health system, a combination
of federal funding of CMHCs, state funding, Medicaid, and Medicare,
started to change. During the 1980s, the federal government turned
over CMHC funding to the states in the form of block grants, and

FIGURE 1   **Who Pays for Health Care?**

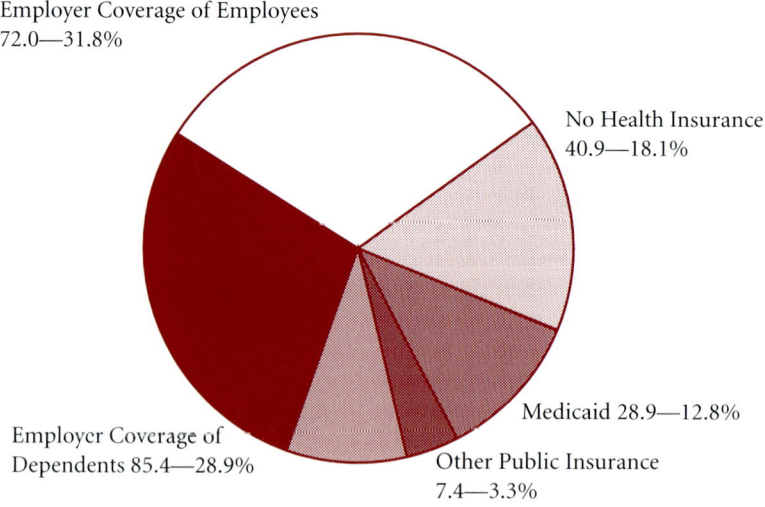

For Non-Elderly Population

Employer Coverage of Employees
72.0—31.8%

No Health Insurance
40.9—18.1%

Medicaid 28.9—12.8%

Employer Coverage of
Dependents 85.4—28.9%

Other Public Insurance
7.4—3.3%

Other Private Insurance
20.8—9.2%

II

many of the original core services were discontinued in the absence of the federal mandates.[6] During the same decade, the Health Care Financing Administration (HCFA), which regulates Medicaid and Medicare, approved the first managed care demonstration projects through its waiver process.[7] The adoption of managed care models, coupled with a move toward privatization, has dramatically changed the public mental health system in most states. These developments are described in greater detail in the next chapter.

[6] Powell, ibid, p. 990.
[7] Oss, M.E. & Moghul, A. Ph.D. "The Managed Behavioral Health Care Industry: Overview and Future Prospects." *1997 Behavioral Managed Care Sourcebook*, New York: Faulkner and Gray, 1996, pp. 3–9.

Medicaid, Other Public Mental Health Systems, and Managed Care

A.   The Medicaid Program and Eligibility Requirements

Medicaid is a federal/state matching entitlement program that provides medical assistance for certain individuals and families with low income or who meet other specific requirements. The $131 billion Medicaid program provides health care for more than 40 million low-income Americans.

Federal Medicaid mandates call for common eligibility and minimum benefit requirements, but states have discretion on how to implement these programs. States generally have broad flexibility in determining which groups their Medicaid programs will cover and the financial criteria for Medicaid eligibility. To be eligible for federal funds, however, states are required to provide Medicaid coverage for most individuals who receive federally assisted income maintenance payments, as well as for related groups not receiving cash payments. Even under the broadest provisions of the federal statute, Medicaid does not provide health care services for very poor people unless they are in one of the groups listed in Figure 2. For people within these groups, low income is only one criterion for Medicaid eligibility; personal resources and assets are also taken into consideration.

Medicaid was initially formulated as a medical care extension of federally funded income maintenance programs for the poor, with an emphasis placed on mothers with dependent children. Recent legislation has expanded the beneficiary population to include low-income pregnant women, children from low-income households, and certain

III

Medicare beneficiaries. Legislative changes regarding Medicaid also
focused on increased access to services, better quality of care, continu-
ation of specific benefits, enhanced outreach programs, and fewer
limitations on services. In 1996, President Clinton's welfare reform
proposal targeted the Aid to Families With Dependent Children
(AFDC) beneficiary population. In return for AFDC beneficiaries
receiving health care benefits (among other supportive services), these
individuals would be compelled to develop a "personal employ-ability
plan," identifying their needs for schooling or technical training, job
searching, or similar preparation directly related to work opportunities.[8]

Medicaid policies that determine eligibility for services are complex
and vary considerably from state to state. An individual who is eligible

---

[8] U.S. Department of Health and Human Services news release. June 14, 1996. For on-line information, contact http://www.acf.dhhs.gov/ACFNews/news/welfref.html.

FIGURE 2   **Medicaid Eligibility Groups**

- Recipients of Aid to Families With Dependent Children (AFDC)
....
- Children under age 6 who meet the state's financial requirements
....
- Pregnant women who meet the state's financial requirements
....
- Supplemental Security Income (SSI) recipients
....
- Recipients of adoption assistance and foster care who are under Title
  IV-E of the Social Security Act
....
- All children born after September 30, 1983, in families with incomes at
  or below the poverty level
....
- Special protected groups (typically individuals who lose AFDC or SSI
  assistance due to earnings from work or increased Social Security
  benefits)
....
- Certain Medicare beneficiaries
....
States also have the option to provide Medicaid coverage for other
"categorically needy" individuals.
....

for Medicaid in one state might not be eligible in another state. More-over, services offered to eligible individuals within a particular state may change during a given year.

B.   Payment Mechanisms and Exemptions of the Medicaid Program

Within the Medicaid system, states pay health care professionals di-rectly. Psychiatrists participating in the Medicaid program must accept the established Medicaid reimbursement level as payment in full. With a few specific exceptions, each state has broad discretion in de-termining (within federally imposed parameters) the reimbursement formula and resulting rate for services.

In addition to the broad discretion states enjoy in determining rates for services, individual states may impose nominal deductibles, co-insurance, or copayments upon some Medicaid recipients for certain services. However, certain Medicaid recipients must be excluded from such cost-sharing measures, including pregnant women, children under age 18, hospital or nursing home patients (who are expected to contribute most of their income to institutional care), and "categori-cally needy" enrollees in Medicaid plans. In addition, recipients re-ceiving emergency and family planning services must be exempt from copayments.

The portion of each state's Medicaid program that is paid by the federal government, known as the Federal Medical Assistance Percent-age (FMAP), is determined annually by a formula that compares the state's average per capita income level with the national income aver-age. By law, the FMAP cannot be lower than 50%, nor can it be higher than 83% of the state's clinical program expenses. Wealthier states have a smaller share of their costs reimbursed. In 1994, the FMAPs varied from 50% (paid to 11 states and the District of Columbia) to 78.9% (paid to Mississippi), with the average federal share among all states being 57.5%. The federal government also shares in the states' administrative expenditures and usually matches 50% of the states'

III

Medicaid administrative expenses. Depending on the complexities and the need for incentives for a particular service, however, higher matching rates may be authorized for certain functions and activities.

Federal Medicaid payments to states have no set limit or "cap"; rather, the federal government matches (at FMAP rates) the state payments for the mandatory services plus the optional services that the individual state decides to provide for eligible recipients. Theoretically, reimbursement rates must be sufficient to guarantee that services offered by Medicaid physicians are comparable to those offered by physicians in the private sector.

States also are required to augment payments made to qualified hospitals that provide inpatient services to a disproportionate number of Medicaid recipients or to other low-income people. Under this system, known as the "disproportionate share hospital" (DSH) program, some states were making large DSH payments in order to receive higher federal matching monies with little or no increases in the individual states' contributions. Because of legislation passed in 1991, however, such DSH payments have become more limited.

C.   Rising Costs of the Medicaid Program

Since its inception, increases in expenditures for the Medicaid program have exceeded the consumer price index. This continually increasing growth in Medicaid expenditures seems to be primarily due to four factors:

- Practitioner payment rates have increased, faster than the rate of inflation;

- There has been an increased use of technologically sophisticated treatment regimens, especially for premature infants and critically ill patients;

- There has been an increase in the number of elderly and disabled covered individuals, subpopulations that require extensive health care services; and

III

- There has been an increase in the overall number of Medicaid-eligible beneficiaries.

Among the Medicaid services offered to beneficiaries, the largest increase has occurred in the area of long-term health care. The Medicaid program has paid for approximately 45% of those individuals utilizing nursing facilities or health services. Medicaid payments for institutional and community-based long-term care totaled almost $46 billion in 1994.

Similarly, public mental health expenditures have risen sharply. Although no specific statistics are available that document the proportion of Medicaid dollars allocated to mental health (i.e., psychiatric and substance abuse care), more attention has been paid to these escalating costs, and efforts to contain them have increased at both the federal and state levels. Financing decisions have therefore been based on the fundamental need to control costs. Factors driving public mental health financing decisions, such as an increase in state autonomy, an increased interest in privatization, and stricter budgets, have set the stage for the implementation of managed care financing models in the public sector.

Total Medicaid Cost, Fiscal Years 1990–1995   FIGURE 3

In Billions of Dollars

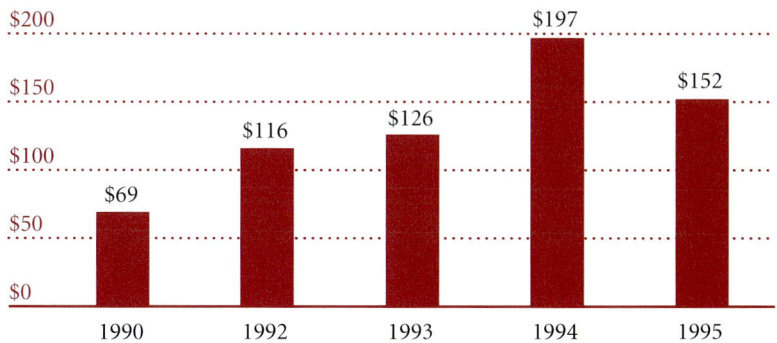

Source: Medicaid Bureau Form HCFA-64 FY 1990–1995; figures have been rounded.

III

D.   The Waiver Phenomenon and the Move Into Managed Care for Mental Health

Since the early 1980s, when the Health Care Financing Administration (HCFA) granted a waiver for the first Medicaid managed care demonstration project, several states have asked for, and received, waivers from HCFA to allow Medicaid recipients to be enrolled in managed care programs, including managed mental health programs. These demonstration projects represented the first application of managed care financing models to a portion of the public mental health system. As of January 1996, 32% of Medicaid beneficiaries were enrolled in some type of managed care plan.

Section 1915(b) and Section 1115 waivers To adopt mandatory managed care models, states must obtain approval from HCFA to waive certain federal Medicaid requirements. Most waiver states are simultaneously seeking authority to use Medicaid funds to provide health care coverage to a portion of their low-income population that is currently ineligible for Medicaid benefits, as well as to implement managed care. States anticipate that savings from capitated managed care systems plus the redirection of other Medicaid or state funds will finance the coverage of these additional beneficiaries. There are two HCFA waivers that most commonly apply to Medicaid managed care: the 1915(b) waiver and the 1115 waiver. The largest difference between 1915(b) waivers and 1115 waivers is in who can and cannot be served. Whereas Section 1115 waivers allow for a complete restructuring of the Medicaid program and an expansion of services to currently uninsured, low-income individuals and families, section 1915(b) waivers are considerably more limited.

As of the mid-1990s, many states have applied for and obtained section 1915(b) waivers. This particular waiver, which allows an exemption from the Medicaid rule allowing recipients complete freedom of practitioner choice, is now being used by 44 states to serve Medicaid recipients.

The waiver authority that gives states the greatest flexibility in implementing statewide managed care programs resides in Section 1115 of

III

the Social Security Act. Herein, the executive branch has been granted broad authority to waive most requirements of the federal statute to facilitate projects likely to further the objectives of the Medicaid program. As part of the process of obtaining a Section 1115 waiver, states must propose a financing plan that, over five years, is intended not to require greater federal expenditures on their Medicaid programs than would have been the case without a waiver. In 1993, in the midst of a national debate over eliminating barriers to health insurance, a handful of states sought Section 1115 waivers from HCFA to simultaneously achieve two related goals: (1) expand coverage to the uninsured, and (2) contain the cost of publicly funded programs by shifting from fee-for-service to managed care–based delivery systems. The stated intent was to permit more individuals to be covered at little or no additional cost through more efficient delivery of medical services. The only prior use of Section 1115 authority comparable to recent statewide waiver applications was the 1982 initiation of a managed care program in Arizona, a state that previously had not participated in Medicaid.

During 1996, the growing number of applications and the interest shown by many states has placed Section 1115 waivers in the center of the debate over how the Medicaid program should evolve. The Clinton Administration has favored linking managed care flexibility to the expansion of Medicaid to previously ineligible groups. At least one recent Section 1115 applicant, however, has asked for greater flexibility to pursue managed care without expanding eligibility.

The statewide Section 1115 waivers, approved and pending, have certain common features: most seek to expand Medicaid coverage to broader populations than those covered under the standard program, and all of the states seeking waivers intend to use mandatory enrollment in capitated managed care plans to better control program spending.

While some states are limiting managed care to the AFDC and AFDC-related populations of women and children, others are expanding managed care to the aged and disabled. This will undoubtedly create new challenges for these states and the participating health plans

III

because these individuals are not normally served by either public or private managed health care plans.

Since 1993, 25 states have sought a statewide section 1115 waiver. However, only four states have actually implemented such waivers. These states include Rhode Island, Tennessee, Oregon, and Hawaii. The disparity between interest in obtaining and the ability to operate under a waiver highlights an important aspect of the Section 1115 phenomenon: implementing these enormously complex and often controversial demonstrations involves addressing issues beyond the normal federal review process.

As more states seek federal approval of a Section 1115 waiver, the time period between waiver submission and approval has lengthened. Five waivers were submitted between November 1992 and June 1993, and each was approved before the end of 1993, with review periods ranging from three to seven months. In 1994, however, only one of the nine waivers pending since the end of 1993 was approved for implementation. Florida's approval took approximately seven months of negotiations with HCFA. This increase in review time appears to be primarily caused by two factors: controversy about some of the implemented demonstrations, and the increasing number of waivers requested.

Concerns have been raised about the rapid approval and implementation of Tennessee's waiver and the state's acknowledged failure to consult with all affected stakeholders, especially physicians. In June 1994, the National Association of Community Health Centers went to court to stop the implementation of statewide Section 1115 waivers, arguing in part that approval was arbitrary and capricious because it failed to consider the views of all interested parties.

HCFA responded to these concerns by publishing principles and procedures to ensure that communities affected by a demonstration project would have adequate opportunity to comment. Another indication of HCFA's intention to respond to these concerns was its November 1994 conditional approval of South Carolina's Section 1115 waiver, with the understanding that HCFA would approve implementation only after the state reached a number of milestones related to the adequacy of service delivery and capitation rates. These issues have been a major and continuing criticism of the Tennessee waiver.

In addition, the number of waivers now pending—10 as of mid-1995—has undoubtedly tested HCFA's review capacity. Furthermore, this backlog is likely to increase. According to HCFA, as many as five additional states are considering potential waivers or are already drafting waiver concept papers. HCFA is establishing an office of state health reform that, together with HCFA regional offices, should more effectively support the development and implementation of statewide Section 1115 waivers.

HCFA approval of a waiver, however, is often only an intermediate step to a state's program implementation because consensus on the waiver design begins at the state level. For example, Florida asked for federal permission to implement its Section 1115 program before obtaining waiver approval from its state legislature. Though approved at the federal level in September 1994, the waiver is only now being debated by the Florida legislature, and the outcome is uncertain. In Kentucky, state legislators doubted that managed care savings would be sufficient to expand coverage to additional groups, and they ultimately refused to authorize implementation of an approved waiver. Kentucky officials informed the General Accounting Office's Health, Education, and Human Services Division that they felt caught in a "Catch 22" because the legislature demanded demonstrated savings before approving planned coverage expansions, and HCFA refused to allow the state to proceed with managed care initiatives unless Kentucky gave a specific date for expanding coverage to new groups. Ohio must also obtain state legislators' approval before implementing its recently approved waiver.

E.   State Policy Issues in Mental Health Financing

Unlike primary health care, mental health care has traditionally presented some unique problems for legislators (see Figure 4). Most state public mental health systems have been dependent on multiple fund-

III

ing sources, including Medicaid, Medicare, program funding, county/ local funding, and the state hospital systems. In addition, there has been a significant overlap of mental health funding with funding for other social services, especially child welfare and corrections. This has meant that there are additional policy issues to be addressed in applying managed care models to public mental health. The five key state policy issues in the application of managed care to the public mental health system are:

- Whether to develop a Medicaid-mental-health-only model or a pooled funding model, where other health and human services funding (such as Medicare) is combined with Medicaid mental health funding.

- Whether to develop an HMO-based or mental health carve-out delivery mechanism.

- Whether to develop the carve-out on a statewide or regional basis, if a carve-out model is chosen.

- What the role of the government entity should be:

  - the government entity may assume the role of provider of mental health services;

FIGURE 4   **Mental Health Presents Unique Problems for State Policy Makers**

Multiple Sources of Funding for Public Mental Health
- Medicaid
- Federal/State Program Funding
- State Hospital System
- County/Local Funding
- Medicare

Overlap of Mental Health Funding With Social Service Funding
- Corrections/Juvenile Justice
- Child Welfare
- Mental Retardation/Developmental Disabilities
- Housing

- the government entity may assume the fiscal risk for the provision of services; or

- the government entity may become the contracting agent selecting and monitoring vendors who provide managed mental health services or clinical services.

■ Whether or not to combine public mental health service money with funding for other services, such as mental retardation, child welfare, and psychotropic pharmacy.

In addition to the policy issues, there are six considerations for legislators in assessing the success of a public managed mental health initiative:

Consolidation Mental health funding streams should be consolidated into a single patient-friendly delivery and financing system.

Parity There should be equal coverage for mental health treatment services.

Mergers When public entities decide to "carve out" mental health benefits, this often involves a merger between the public system and private mental health benefit carve-out companies. The inherent differences between the public and private systems must be addressed.

Cost-shifting Legislators should consider the effects of cost-shifting from managed Medicaid systems to other areas of state spending.

Safety net In general, eligibility-driven, capitated systems have a "built-in" safety system for beneficiaries. All eligible beneficiaries who present for treatment must be treated within a capitated system.

Experience In general, state governments lack experience in contracting and monitoring vendors.

E.1. Medicaid Mental Health Only vs. Pooled Funding Model

A fundamental policy decision for legislators is whether to design a public managed mental health program that includes only Medicaid

III

mental health funding or incorporates some part of state mental health program funds. HCFA waiver approval is generally more rapid if only Medicaid funds are at issue, and such programs usually result in Medicaid cost savings. Such program designs, however, create two public mental health systems with duplicate administrative costs, difficulty in coordinating patient care, and possible cost-shifting to program funded mental health programs.

Conversely, a pooled funding plan would combine Medicaid mental health funds with state funding for mental health services to create a single public mental health delivery system. Advocates for such pooled funding models argue that such models create a seamless pool of funding for patients. Critics, however, point out that there are few managed health models with experience managing the broad range of public mental health services, that data do not exist for appropriate rate estimation, and that such models eliminate the public mental health safety net, particularly for low-income employed individuals who have little or no mental health insurance coverage but have income making them ineligible for public services.

For psychiatrists, the two funding options can have some distinct results. Medicaid-only managed mental health models can have the effect of creating two public mental health systems—one composed of psychiatrists and other practitioners who have contracts with the entity selected to manage care on behalf of the state, and the other composed of programs that receive state program funding. This can make coordination of patient care difficult. On the other hand, pooled funding models create issues for adequate mental health services for working individuals with inadequate mental health coverage. With the elimination of the traditional safety net, psychiatrists may be faced with ethical issues about ensuring appropriate continuing care when access to the public mental health system is limited, particularly for individuals with serious mental illnesses.

E.2.   The Carve-Out Issue

A "carve-out" approach to mental health financing separates the funds for mental health services from general medical funding, creating a separate plan for its management. With regard to whether or not to carve out mental health services, state policy makers should consider several advantages and disadvantages. The advantages of a carve-out include:

- The relative lack of experience of general medical managed care organizations (MCOs) in providing public mental health services is compensated by utilizing a carve-out program. Approximately half of all HMOs currently carve out their mental health benefits.

- The inherent "medical model" orientation of combined benefit plans is minimized.

- The tendency to divert or under-fund mental health services that are found in combined benefit plans is mitigated.

- Direct access to mental health services is provided.

One of the major disadvantages of engaging a carve-out for mental health services is the creation of artificial boundaries between "health" and "mental health." Under such boundaries, psychiatrists are not allowed to render certain services (e.g., prescribe medications, order some tests, etc.) which are classified as belonging to "health" as opposed to "mental health." Such an artificial boundary should be questioned in light of the increased use of psychopharmaceuticals in the psychiatric profession. Other disadvantages of using a carve-out for public mental health services include:

- The potential lack of integration with the primary health care practitioners and payers;

- The potential restriction of patient choice of practitioners;

- The possible duplication of administrative staff and tasks; and

- The possibility of patient confusion due to program differences (e.g., utilization review and claims processes, copayments and deductibles, etc.) between the primary health care plan and the mental health carve-out.

III

E.3.   The Role of the State Government

Several issues concerning the role of state government become relevant, including whether state governments should assume the financial risk for mental health benefits or whether that risk should be privatized. The advantages of the state government entity retaining financial risk include:

- Cost-shifting across systems may be easier to manage and/or prevent; and

- Under-funded systems have historically been targets of "profit making"—government control of these services would minimize this.

The disadvantages include:

- Patient advocacy is easier when the public sector is the purchaser of services;

- Public systems lack the capital for necessary system investment; and

- Government entities may not be efficient in fiscal management because leadership may derive from political appointments. Such positions, by definition, do not afford stability, and the individuals filling them may not be the most qualified.

E.4.   Pooled Funding Streams Beyond Mental Health

As state governments consider managed care models for mental health, one policy consideration that arises is the potential for cost-shifting to other areas of social service funding such as child welfare, housing assistance, or services for the mentally retarded or developmentally disabled. For this reason, some states (e.g., Kansas, Pennsylvania, Wisconsin) have implemented demonstration projects that have included some funding from other areas of social service that have been traditionally quite distinct from mental health. State managed care programs that pool these multiple social service funding streams have been difficult because of the requirements for federal waivers.

Some Congressional proposals to allow the blending of current block
grant programs into Medicaid, and possibly delivering all federal
health care funding for the poor to individual states as much larger
block grants, would make these pooled arrangements much more
common. Block grants deliver large amounts of money to states to use
within certain specified categorical guidelines. There are currently
nine federal block grant programs, delivering funds for 58 different
categorical programs. The federal block grant program for mental
health totaled $290 million 1994, and is estimated to be more than
$275 million in 1995. Federal block grant money for substance abuse
services in 1994 totaled $1.16 billion, and is estimated at $1.23 billion in
1995.[9] The presumed advantage to the states is increased flexibility on
how to spend the federal funds.

Advocates maintain that the advantages of pooling funding streams
under managed care models include:

- **Integration of funding for special populations.** Currently, seriously
  mentally ill individuals require a broad array of social services,
  from psychiatric services to housing assistance to supplemental
  income. Theoretically, pooled funding arrangements allow more
  flexibility in allocating these resources.

- **Preventing cost-shifting across "silos of funding."** As mentioned
  earlier in this section, capitated managed care plans can create
  a scenario where cost-shifting between funding services occurs.

- **The reduction of government administration expense.** Advocates
  argue that large, multi-program funding pools can be managed by
  a single managed care entity, greatly decreasing government administrative expenses.

Opponents of these proposed pooled funding streams have several
concerns:

---

[9] Office of the Actuary, Office of National Health Statistics, U.S. Department of Health and Human
Services.

III

- **Potential political issues of control and consolidation among both service agencies and health care professionals.** Pooled funding models collapse multiple agencies' discretion over funding, consolidating control and allocation of resources.

- **The creation of competition between advocacy groups of "special" populations.** Many constituency groups fear that state pooled funding plans would eliminate ear-marked funds for particular populations and leave the most vulnerable groups with a smaller proportion of total funds.

- **The lack of previously existing precedents for pricing, operations, and outcomes.** From a practical perspective, opponents of pooled funding models point out there is a lack of history and experience for wide-scale implementation.

For psychiatrists, proposed pooled funding models have a number of implications. From a patient care planning perspective, integration of funding streams should permit more flexible planning, particularly for seriously mentally ill individuals. However, the financial incentives of the managed care program, prospective authorization processes, and lack of state performance benchmarks can prevent this flexibility from being a reality. Another concern is that of advocacy for seriously mentally ill individuals. Services for these individuals have historically been underfunded. The prospect of pooling these funds with other social service dollars raises the prospect of a further erosion of service levels for this vulnerable population.

F.   Factors Affecting the Success of Applying Managed Care to Public Mental Health

Two factors seem to significantly affect the degree to which a state's Medicaid managed care program succeeds in meeting its goals of controlling costs while improving access to quality care implementation: (1) how much time the state allows for planning and execution,

and (2) oversight of clinical, administrative, and financial performance.

F.1.   Implementation

State initiatives for managed mental health care involve substantial
changes for all constituencies involved—patients, state Medicaid and
mental health program managers, and psychiatrists. As discussed in
detail in other monographs in this series, managed care changes referral patterns, access to service, payment amounts and terms, financial
incentives, and benefit plans.

From a patient perspective, patients and their advocates need to un-
derstand the new managed care systems. Of particular import are
issues affecting access to care (both preauthorization requirements and
provider network composition) and appeals processes. State policy
makers and staff need to develop sufficient systems and staff expertise
for oversight of new managed care initiatives.

For many psychiatrists, a state's decision to move its public mental
health system to a managed care financing and delivery model may
have a number of effects that demand adequate time for implementation. As discussed in *The Psychiatrist's Guide to Managed Care Contracting*, managed care contracts demand significant changes in the
operation of psychiatric groups—from information systems to staffing
to clinical pathways. In addition, traditional clinical case management
methods, preferred clinical practices, and authorized service providers
may change as well. Psychiatric practices need time to respond to
these changes.

Operating a wide-scale managed care program differs significantly
from the traditional fee-for-service programs. Implementing a program
more slowly allows time to acquire staff expertise, develop a community base of support, create an organizational structure and administrative operation, and properly educate staff, practitioners, and
beneficiaries. Planning and implementation are facilitated in a state
with widespread managed care in the private sector because the mem-

bers of the community, particularly practitioners, are already familiar with managed care.

F.2.   Oversight

The degree to which appropriate oversight mechanisms are in place has significant impact on the operation of a public managed care system. Quality improvement systems, including patient satisfaction surveys, are particularly important to ensure that beneficiaries are receiving sufficient care of acceptable quality. Financial incentives to under-serve are inherent to managed care and may lead to problems. Large private sector employers have recognized the importance of oversight in this area and are demanding strong quality improvement systems in health plans throughout the country.

State oversight of a managed care program cannot be effective, particularly in the area of quality improvement, without good data collection efforts and information systems to report beneficiaries' experiences. Information systems are generally new, since the information needs of a state with a managed care program are different from those with a fee-for-service program.

Another important oversight function is the financial review of health plans' solvency and allocation of revenues. The financial condition of a plan can have a strong impact on the access to and quality of care. Moreover, the plan must ensure that program dollars are used primarily for health services and that management and administrative expenses are limited.

Medicare and Managed Care

Medicare has not been exempt from the transition to managed care. By the mid-1970s, managed care organizations, primarily HMOs, began to demand a modification of the Medicare fee-for-service orientation. Ultimately, a compromise was reached between fee-for-service advocates and the managed care organizations, and by the end of the 1970s, the Medicare risk contract was born.

A.   Eligibility Requirements of the Medicare Program

Initially, the Medicare program was designed to cover people age 65 and over. In 1973, the entitlement was expanded to include people who had been disabled for Social Security purposes for two years, as well as a small percentage of people with end-stage renal disease. People under 65 who are suffering from serious mental illness are eligible for Medicare Part A benefits (inpatient and hospital outpatient care) if they meet the following criteria: (1) they have collected Social Security Disability Income for 24 months, and (2) they have contributed to the Social Security system for defined periods of time based on their age and years worked before they became eligible for disability benefits.

B.   Rising Costs and Payment Mechanisms of the Medicare Program

By the mid-1970s, Medicare costs began to increase enormously, and efforts were undertaken to bring these costs under control without

IV

limiting services. In 1995, there were about 36.9 million Americans enrolled in this program, with a total expenditure of about $177 billion (see figure below). By the turn of the century, Medicare costs are expected to exceed $314 billion.

According to recent statistics, enrollments in Medicare HMOs have been increasing substantially.[10] In 1994, 15 states (including California, New York, and Florida, states with significant Medicare-eligible populations) saw an increase of at least 10% in voluntary Medicare HMO enrollees. In that same year, 20% of Medicare beneficiaries in California, Arizona, Oregon, and Hawaii were enrolled in HMOs, and an additional six states (including Florida) had from 6% to 19% of Medi-

---

[10] C. Keith Powell & John H. Straub. Medicare Managed Care Manual. New York: Thompson Publishing Group, Tab 300, p. 6, 1996.

FIGURE 5   **Trends and Projected Growth in Medicare Costs**

Estimates by HCFA actuaries; figures have been rounded up.

In Billions of Dollars

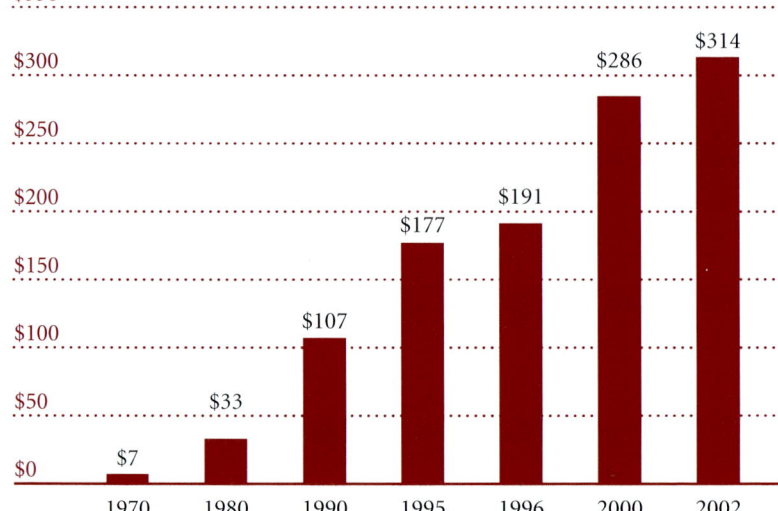

Source: Health Care Financing Administration, Bureau of Data Management and Strategy, Office of Health Care Information Systems, Report Date March 1996, Congressional Budget Office, January 1997.

care beneficiaries enrolled in HMOs. Clearly, the number of Medicare enrollees within managed care entities is significant and undoubtedly will continue to grow, which will have a direct and profound impact on psychiatrists who treat this particular population.

C.   HMOs and Medicare

An HMO is an organization that is often described as a prepaid health plan. It is considered the most restrictive of managed care models because of its use of primary care physicians as referral physicians who decide what health services the patients need and when. A Medicare HMO is one that has been approved by HCFA to provide managed care benefits to qualified beneficiaries who would otherwise receive self-referred Medicare benefits on a fee-for-service basis. HMOs have traditionally viewed their Medicare plans as competitive commercial products, marketing aggressively to individuals and retiree groups. HMO benefit packages enhance standard Medicare benefits by providing additional benefits and/or by paying copayments and deductibles that would otherwise be the responsibility of the beneficiary.

There are two basic payment arrangements an HMO may enter into with HCFA: a Medicare risk contract or a Medicare cost contract.

Under a Medicare risk contract, the beneficiary assigns all of his or her benefits to the HMO, and the HMO assumes the risk for payment of all services. The beneficiary must then receive all services from the HMO's panel of practitioners, and the HMO pays all of the usual Medicare copayments and deductibles that the beneficiary would have been responsible for paying.

Under a Medicare cost contract, the beneficiary retains his or her Medicare benefit option. The implication is that if the beneficiary uses the HMO's panel of practitioners, all services including copayments and deductibles are covered and paid in full. The beneficiary, however, may seek care outside of the HMO practitioner panel and receive services from any practitioner who accepts Medicare reimbursement. In such instances, the practitioner bills Medicare, not the HMO, and

IV

the beneficiary is responsible for applicable copayments and deductibles.

Because of the increase in management of Medicare populations, psychiatrists treating this population will need to become familiar with the concepts inherent to risk-based financing mechanisms, especially capitation. Risk-based and capitation contracts are more thoroughly discussed in the next chapter, as well as in *The Psychiatrist's Guide to Managed Care Contracting* and *The Psychiatrist's Guide to Capitation and Risk-Based Contracting*, both part of this series.

D.   Relationship Between Medicare and Medicaid

One of the major issues within both the Medicare and Medicaid programs is the treatment of people with serious mental illness. Many of these individuals are eligible for Medicaid by virtue of their income and eligible for Medicare by virtue of their disability.

According to research conducted by *OPEN MINDS*, an estimated 35% of individuals with schizophrenia in the United States were in managed care plans by the close of 1996. Such dually eligible individuals pose particular problems as both the Medicare and Medicaid programs transition to managed care models. In states where this managed care adoption rate is great, there appear to be three main issues relating to Medicare-eligible individuals whose benefits are capitated in both the Medicare and Medicaid programs, discussed below:

Copayments and premium payments Medicare has developed the rates for Medicare HMO enrollees based on actual cost-related experience, and in Medicare cost contracts these rates have been reduced based on expected collections from beneficiaries of copayments and premium payments. Medicaid, however, does not allow patients to be billed or required to pay any copayments or premiums. In the case of beneficiaries who are dually eligible, Medicare HMO cost contract plans have had their rates reduced to reflect expected copayments but are unable to bill the patient because of the Medicaid rules.

Coordination of benefits A problem may potentially occur when a patient presents to a psychiatrist for an assessment and the psychiatrist subsequently determines that the patient requires additional services. In one scenario, the Medicaid HMO may disallow the services as not medically necessary, sometimes using a different set of criteria than the Medicare managed mental health program. In another scenario, the psychiatrist may not be part of the Medicare HMO practitioner network, but may be part of the Medicaid managed mental health program's practitioner network. In both scenarios, there usually is little reciprocal coordination of benefits between the Medicare HMO and the Medicaid HMO.

Establishment of appropriate rates The mental health capitation rates for dually eligible seriously mentally ill individuals in Medicaid managed mental health programs were developed assuming a certain recovery of funds through coordination of benefits with Medicare. This recovery of funds generally declines as the proportion of these individuals enrolled in Medicare HMOs (as opposed to fee-for-service programs) increases. Such rates must be adjusted as this proportion changes.

Special Considerations for the Care of Individuals With Serious Mental Illnesses

One of the areas generating the most concern and controversy in managed public mental health programs is the care of those with a chronic or serious mental illness. Although the description, "seriously mentally ill," implies a defined, targeted group, there continues to be a variety of approaches for defining, treating, and providing financing for this population.

A.   Definition of "Serious Mental Illness"

A variety of approaches are commonly used to define the population having serious mental illness. The approaches can be summarized as follows:

- **The diagnostic approach** (i.e., people with schizophrenia, psychotic mood disorders, etc.);

- **The utilization approach** (i.e., targeting high utilizers of service or institutionalized patients); and

- **Definition- or criteria-driven approach** A common definition for serious mental illness is "a diagnosable mental disorder that is sufficiently severe and enduring as to cause functional impairment in one or more life areas and often recurrent need for mental health services."[11] An example of the criteria-driven approach is

---

[11] "Concept Paper: Mental Health and Substance Abuse Managed Care." 1997 *Mental Managed Care Sourcebook*, Faulkner and Gray, 1996, p. 279.

V

that used in the HCFA waiver application for Special Needs Plans submitted by the State of New York.[12] In this approach, the chronically mentally ill eligible for membership in a Special Needs Plan are:

1. People who, within the preceding 12 months, have been discharged from intermediate (31–90 day) or long (more than 90 days) stays in state psychiatric hospitals and residential treatment facilities;

2. Participants in intensive case management or supportive case management programs;

3. People enrolled in licensed partial hospitals, day treatment (children), continuing day treatment (adults), and intensive psychiatric rehabilitation programs; and

4. People with three or more hospital admissions for a mental health problem or five or more emergency room visits related to a psychiatric incident in the preceding 12 months.

Whatever the definition or classification, there is wide agreement that publicly funded mental health systems have borne the significant burden of care for this population. CMHCs have been associated with a mandate to facilitate the elimination of state mental hospitals, implying that their caseloads will be dominated by severely mentally ill patients. It should be noted that the CMHCs may potentially see more functionally impaired cases as well, further increasing the burden of publicly funded mental health systems. Clearly, the publicly funded mental health system will continue to play an increasingly larger role in the treatment of seriously mentally ill individuals.

B.   Access to Care

Of the many criticisms leveled at managed care, the one most often cited for those with chronic illnesses has been access to care. Section

---

[12] Henry Yennie & Monica E. Oss. "New York City SMI/SMP Rates: Between $10K and $12K." *OPEN MINDS*, 1997, Vol. 11, No. 1, p. 12.

V

1302 of the HMO Act, which describes the coverage HMOs must offer as basic services to be designated as federally qualified, permits HMOs to limit treatment of mental illness. The HMO Act requires HMOs to offer 20 outpatient visits, stipulates no basic health service requirement for inpatient treatment, and requires outpatient treatment only for "evaluative and crisis intervention mental health services." This permits, by inference, exclusion of chronic mental illness from mental health benefit coverage. The mechanism often used to provide care for those patients excluded from traditional HMOs was cost-shifting to the public sector. As the public sector moves toward managed care itself, however, there are fewer and fewer opportunities to cost-shift the care of this population.

Some health care experts maintain that HMOs are uniquely structured to treat chronic patients, including patients suffering from chronic mental illness. However, there are few public or private precedents for adding seriously mentally ill individuals to managed care programs. The states that have moved in this direction are in the process of conducting the first formal evaluations of these demonstration projects.

C.   Financing Treatment for the Seriously Mentally Ill

Treatment of the seriously mentally ill population often requires long-term coordinated care. Such coordinated care is, at best, difficult in the traditional public system with its fragmented and restrictive program funding. This fragmentation is cited as producing inefficiencies, duplication, poor use of resources, and failure to serve patients in need.[13] Specifically, such fragmentation produces the following:

- Funding tied to specific institutions and/or professionals, which prevents adaptation of service settings and treatment to meet individual needs;

---

[13] Mechanic, D. & Aiken, L. Capitation in Mental Health: Potentials and Cautions. "Paying for Services" [Promises and Pitfalls of Capitation: *New Directions for Mental Health Services*], No. 43. San Francisco: Jossey-Bass, 1989.

V

- People with severe mental illness who are more prone than other users of the health system to be derailed by the confusing maze of practitioners and eligibility rules and who often "fall through the cracks;" and

- Practitioners who may attempt to shift costs onto each other and provide inappropriate treatment in the process.

D.   Financing Psychotropic Medications for Serious Mental Illnesses

The costs of medications in both public and private systems have traditionally been separated from the funding of services. Recent developments in the public sector are indicating a shift of this cost responsibility to the service clinician.

The two most notable programs addressing this combined funding approach for mental health service and psychotropic medication are the TennCare Program in Tennessee and the proposed Special Needs Plans in New York. Under TennCare, the behavioral health organization is capitated not only for the provision of services but also for the cost of psychotropic medications. The proposed New York Special Needs Plans is calling for the inclusion of the cost of Clozaril® and similar high-cost antipsychotics in the capitation rate for services.

These programs represent a new trend in capitation financing for the public mental health system and present the following new challenges as follows:

- The accumulation and analysis of pharmaceutical usage data from sources not previously accessed by mental health clinicians;

- The use of this data in the establishment of capitation rates and the management of the increased financial risk associated with this new responsibility;

- The development of new protocols for evaluation of new compounds and their efficacy in the treatment of mental illness in a capitated environment with fixed revenue streams;

V

- A knowledge of and an influence in the design and maintenance of formularies to control costs and support clinical pathways;

- New partnerships with pharmaceutical manufacturers to gain access to disease management protocols, pharmaceutical discounts, and distribution channels; and

- The design of new mechanisms for coordination with somatic medicine and primary care physicians.

This trend is also being observed in the private sector as managed care companies are introducing "integrated" mental health benefit management/pharmaceutical management products. These trends in psychotropic medication funding will have profound implications for psychiatrists practicing within the public mental health system. With the increased focus on risk-based financing, accountability, and cost-containment within both the public and private sectors, psychiatrists will undoubtedly be encouraged to follow clinical pathways that save money.

E.   The Care of Children With Serious Emotional Disturbance

England and Cole (1993) eloquently cite the particular challenges of and system shortcomings for seriously emotionally disturbed children. They write, "Ironically, the fundamental problem of child and family mental health care in this country is that our public policy for child and family mental health has itself fallen through the cracks. . . . Somehow we have backed into a policy . . . that is, in every respect, perverse. We have artificially limited the traditional mental health benefit so that it runs out close to the time when it is most needed. This can leave a critical hiatus in care just as a child's condition goes from bad to worse and as a family's tolerance and strength are most vulnerable. Public funding is withheld until there is a full-blown crisis and the home situation has fallen apart. Then these resources are divided unevenly among five or six public agencies, none of which, by itself, is equipped to provide intensive care and all of which have a great incentive to shift responsibility to other agencies."[14]

The move to managed care for public sector programs with the responsibility for children's mental health poses significant risks and opportunities as follows:

- Managed care funding may drive some traditional children's service agencies out of business due to duplication, inefficiency, and resistance to change.

- Managed care presents a true opportunity to coordinate services and address the issues of "crisis management" so common in children's mental health services. In addition, managed care provides an opportunity to develop new services to fill service gaps in order to create a true continuum of care.

- The inclusion of children's services in public managed care efforts presents the opportunity to bring children's mental health issues to the mainstream of U.S. health care policy.

There are also trends and challenges unique to managed care efforts targeting mental health services for children with serious emotional disturbance:

- A major trend is the inclusion of traditional social services in mental health Medicaid managed care programs. Long considered two separate systems, the marriage of mental health services and social services in several states is a growing trend. Some states, including West Virginia, Georgia, and California, have proposed the inclusion of foster care and other social service programs in the "carve-out" programs for Medicaid funds. Other states, including Wisconsin and Kansas, are considering proposals for privatizing long-term care and foster care, respectively. Some counties in Ohio are considering proposals for integrating care

---

[14] England, M. & Cole, R. "Children and Mental Health: How Can the System Be Improved?" *Health Affairs*, 1993, Vol. 14, No. 3, p. 131.

V

management, funding, and practitioner networks for child welfare, mental health, and substance abuse.

- Unlike traditional mental health programs for adults, the court is a key stakeholder in the children's mental health service system. The role of courts and justice systems in the care of seriously emotionally disturbed children is complex and often overlooked in managed care reform efforts. Anecdotal evidence from states such as Tennessee and Iowa suggests a continuing lack of coordination between the managed mental health clinician charged with delivering and financing services, the courts charged with mandating placements and services, and the social service agencies charged with coordinating the array of services needed for care and protection of these children and their families.

- Also somewhat unique to children's services is the presence of court mandates and orders of supervision. Resulting from a variety of sources including lawsuits, class action judgments, and legislation, these various mandates often dictate the mix of access and services to be delivered by the public agencies responsible for the care of seriously emotionally disturbed children. These mandates are often at odds with the design and operating principles of managed care programs.

- The role of the educational system in the care of children with serious emotional disturbance is also paramount. The integration of educational funds, mental health funds, juvenile justice funds, and social service funds represents uncharted territory in managed care initiatives. The lack of experience in managed care for children's services coupled with the diverse, often competing objectives of these various funding sources places significant risk on the public practitioner managing these initiatives.

- The development of integrated program carve-outs and comprehensive case rates often places unfamiliar and significant risk on agencies that have formerly relied on grants, fee-for-service payments, and charitable contributions. This presents a significant risk for failure and dissolution of long-standing service providers in the community.

It should be noted that the key stakeholders within the children's mental health system may have different funding contingencies (e.g., there exists an unstable tax base for education, as opposed to juvenile justice). This could complicate fiscal integration, and therefore, service integration.

In summary, the financing of services for seriously emotionally disturbed children shares many of the same pitfalls and opportunities as for seriously mentally ill adults. Significant differences exist, however, in the social and justice system environments that place increased risk on the public system for children as it moves to managed care programs. Moreover, the lack of data or experience in managed care initiatives within the public child welfare system implies a "brave new world" for the psychiatrist treating this population.

Performance Measures in Public Mental Health

As states move to managed care models for their public mental health systems, patient advocates fear that decisions about programs will be made only on the basis of spending reductions and not on the basis of value to taxpayers and patients. To ensure that public purchasers receive the highest potential benefit from mental health funds in managed models and to provide a platform for evaluating managed mental health program performance, state purchasers must build performance indicators into contracts with managed mental health delivery systems.

A.   Performance Indicators

There are some existing models for the application of quantifiable performance measures in managed mental health programs. A recent survey of purchasers by *OPEN MINDS* found that these performance indicators fall into five categories: patient/customer satisfaction, administrative proficiency, clinical quality, financial performance and incentives, and cost-shifting considerations. These are described as below:

A.1.   Patient/Customer Satisfaction

Quantifiable performance indicators within the area of patient satisfaction include the collection of specific patient survey data. Such data measure disease, demographic factors (e.g., age, ethnicity, and gender), and geographic location. Other performance indicators within this field include the processing of patient appeals, notably the amount, characteristics, and disposition of appeals.

A.2.   Administrative Proficiency
Quantifiable administrative performance standards include time to appointment/clinical intervention for emergent, urgent, and routine cases; toll-free telephone access (measurements on busy time, abandoned calls, etc.); claims payment accuracy and turnaround time; and appeals resolution time.

A.3.   Clinical Quality
The following quantifiable benchmarks of clinical quality have been established: recidivism and relapse rates (specific to disease, demographic factors, and geographic location); lag time between end of acute/residential treatment and contact with community-based program; consistency of clinical case management criteria application; and improved patient quality of life/functionality.

A.4.   Financial Performance and Incentives
The fourth area of quantifiable performance indicators covers the realm of financial performance and incentives. These parameters include utilization per covered life; residential diversion rates (both immediate and six months post-diversion); the cost per covered life (pre-vendor and post-vendor); appropriation of funds by treatment modality; and appropriate access to care (i.e., a measure of the percentage of the population served within a year).

A.5.   Cost-Shifting Considerations
State purchasers are building performance benchmarks, along with financial penalties and incentives, into the contracts with selected managed mental health programs to address cost-shifting issues among various publicly funded sources. Clinicians and patients should insist on this level of accountability in the expenditure of public funds. Performance indicators that can aid in the measurement of this accountability include changes in the rate of incarceration of mental health patients; changes in the amount of residential service and mental health treatment dollars in the child welfare system; and changes in mental health–related spending by educational programs.

VI

B.   Demonstration Projects

To illustrate the performance indicators currently used in demonstration projects, the specific reporting standards implemented by the
Commonwealth of Pennsylvania and the State of Iowa are described
in this section. The APA is concerned that these efforts are only a
starting point and that decision makers need to expand their efforts to
include a variety of issues, including cultural competence, prevention,
attention to substance abuse, and wrap-around services. Contact the
APA's Office of Economic Affairs and Practice Management for information on the status of public managed care systems guidelines,
which are near completion at the time of printing.

B.1.   Pennsylvania

In the Spring of 1996, the Commonwealth of Pennsylvania issued a
request for proposals (RFP) to the City of Philadelphia and the four
surrounding suburban counties for the management of all public
mental health services in southeastern Pennsylvania. The HealthChoice
RFP specifically stipulated the following performance and outcome
measuring criteria:

Increase community services To achieve this performance standard, the
counties would have to decrease mental health inpatient hospitaliza-
tions, decrease criminal incarcerations, decrease delinquency placements, decrease out-of-home placements, and decrease homelessness.

Increase vocational and educational status This performance indicator
would include increasing school attendance and retention, and increasing the vocational status for adults.

Reduce criminal and delinquent activity This performance parameter
includes reducing the number of arrests, reducing positive drug
screens, improving probation and parole status, and reducing status
offenses, with a focus on truancy.

Improve health care This rather broad performance parameter includes
meeting or exceeding early periodic screening and diagnostic treatment (EPSDT) screening targets set forth by the state, increasing the

number of patients receiving annual physical exams, and reducing hospital emergency room use.

Increase penetration rates The various counties would be required to monitor utilization rates by priority group and type of service, as well as by age group and type of service.

Increase patient and family satisfaction The counties would be able to exercise their discretion in the implementation and monitoring of this performance standard.

Implement continuous quality improvement (CQI) actions The counties were directed to implement systems, policies, and processes to improve efficiencies and patient/family satisfaction.

Increase the range of services and improve utilization patterns Included in this performance criterion is improving the array of treatment, support, and rehabilitative service options; decreasing the number of patients utilizing emergency room and/or inpatient services as their primary access to medical care; reducing the inpatient hospitalization rate; reducing the rate of perinatal addictive disorders; and reducing the overall "drop-out" rate.

Clearly, the performance standards outlined in Pennsylvania's HealthChoice program will pose unique challenges to the city and county governments in the implementation and monitoring of these performance and outcomes criteria.

B.2.   Iowa

The State of Iowa has the distinction of implementing one of the first managed mental health carve-out programs in the nation. Named the Mental Health Access Plan (MHAP), this program includes several performance measurement parameters within the first year of its contract with a private managed mental health care vendor. These performance indicators have increased approximately threefold as the state has renewed and lengthened its contract with its vendor. Some of these specific performance indicators include:

- 15% of service expenditures within the contract year will be spent on services not previously funded by previous fee-for-service Medicaid programs;

- Based on claims paid, services will be provided to an average of 5% of MHAP enrollees each month;

- Based on claims paid, the private vendor will serve at least 15% of enrollees per year;

- 98% of enrollees who request a mental health service will receive authorization for care;

- All new enrollees will receive information on MHAP within 10 days of the receipt of the enrollment tape;

- Educational information will be provided to enrollees at least once per contract year;

- Based on patient satisfaction surveys, 85% of respondents will indicate satisfaction with MHAP services;

- 75% of all authorized units of service will be for service provided outside of a 24-hour setting;

- The average length of inpatient stay will not exceed the fee-for-service average of 12 days;

- Based on clinical outcome assessment scales, those patients who utilize mental health services will show an overall improvement in functioning;

- The rate of readmissions will not exceed 28% within a 60-day time period;

- A minimum of 1000 joint case planning sessions will take place with the physicians during the contract year;

- 80% of the claims will be processed within 30 days, 90% within 60 days, and 100% within 90 days;

- The percentage of claims denied due to vendor error will not exceed 8%;

VI

- Contracts will be processed within 30 days of receipt of the required information; and

- The clinicians must be credentialed within 75 days of receipt of the required information.

Pennsylvania and Iowa have taken the initiative to include performance benchmarks in their public sector mental health care carve-outs. As this monograph goes to press, the Commonwealth of Massachusetts has implemented a preliminary set of performance indicators in the contracts with its managed health care vendor. Whether or not additional state governments impose such performance indicators in their Medicaid behavioral health contracts will depend on the success of the initiatives under way in Pennsylvania, Iowa, and Massachusetts.

The APA is lobbying and educating decision makers on various additional areas of consideration related to performance indicators.

The Changing Role of Psychiatry in Public Mental Health

Public mental health is undergoing change that is significantly affecting the practice of psychiatry. In the decade following World War II, the mentally ill, particularly those with severe disabling mental illnesses, who could not afford private care were more often than not housed in state mental institutions. These state institutions were primarily psychiatry's domain. By the mid-1950s, however, a movement away from mental hospitals was under way. The predominant, though contested, explanation for this change was the discovery and introduction of the major tranquilizers.[15]

As state mental hospitals began to downsize, the majority of psychiatrists who had staffed these institutions moved their practices to the outpatient arena. Another significant institution was also in the early stages of evolution in the mid-1950s. This was the concept of community psychiatry, which evolved into the community mental health center approach to treating public patients during the 1960s.

There were a number of other major events during the years between 1960 and 1980 that made significant impacts on the psychiatric profession. Group health insurance began to allow coverage for some mental conditions; the number of psychologists and social workers in the private practice of psychotherapy increased significantly; and the private, for-profit psychiatric hospital industry boomed.

---

[15] Starr, Paul. *The Social Transformation of American Medicine.* New York: Basic Books, Inc., 1982.

VII

A.   Increased Use of Psychotropic Medications

Psychopharmacology is changing the mental health field and the practice of psychiatry in particular. There are three developments in psychopharmacology that have been most influential: an increasing
awareness of the physiological basis for many mental disorders, an
increase in the number and efficacy of psychotropic drugs, and the
maturation of the disease management concept.

Extensive research into the causes of severe mental illnesses such
as schizophrenia, bipolar disorder, major depression, obsessive-
compulsive disorder, and panic disorder is producing strong evidence
that biological factors are involved. This has led to the investment of a
significant amount of money in research into physiological-based
solutions to mental illness. That research has produced a myriad of
drugs to combat mental disorders. Antidepressants alone are an $8
billion industry. Most important, use of these pharmaceuticals appears
to both improve patient outcomes and reduce cost. Their ability to
reduce treatment costs will most likely cause the managed mental
health care companies to strongly promote the use of pharmaceuticals
in the treatment of serious mental illnesses.

The increase in the prevalence of psychotropic pharmaceuticals has
influenced a managed care technology known as disease management.
This is essentially an integrated system of customized interventions,
measurements, and refinements to current care processes that are
designed to optimize clinical and economic outcomes with a specific
disease state, such as depression. This model for integrating the management and financing of problem-specific patient treatment services
and pharmacy encourages efficacious patient monitoring, particularly
of medication utilization, to control costs.

B.   Reductions in Payments to Psychiatrists

There are a number of different types of financial arrangements that
psychiatrists may enter into with managed care organizations, all of

which involve some form of adjustment in compensation levels. One of the more common ways managed care has reduced the amount psychiatrists are paid is by negotiating discounted contracts with them. In exchange for this discount, the psychiatrist is eligible to receive referrals from the MCO's patient population.

C.   Limited Approval for Long-Term Treatment

Because of its emphasis on cost savings, managed care continues to be quite skeptical of any type of long-term treatment. Psychotherapy, in particular, has received enormous scrutiny. Proponents of managed care have argued that short-term therapy in conjunction with medication can achieve essentially the same outcome at a significantly lower cost. The foundation of this debate falls within the concept of "medical necessity," and whether or not psychotherapies constitute "treatments that are appropriate and necessary to the symptoms, diagnosis, or manifestations of a mental disorder."

D.   Adoption of Universal Rates for Psychotherapy by Some Managed Care Vendors

Under significant pressure to reduce their prices, some managed care organizations are beginning to adopt universal rates (the same rate for a service such as psychotherapy, regardless of the discipline of the individual mental health professional). The APA's Managed Care Committee, Office of Economic Affairs and Practice Management, and leadership are currently combating these universal rate policies, which do not acknowledge the higher training and skill level of the psychiatrist.

E.   Increased Use of Primary Care Physicians Instead of Psychiatrists

Many managed care organizations argue that with appropriate clinical guidelines, primary care physicians (PCPs) can prescribe and monitor psychiatric drugs as effectively as psychiatrists. The tendency for psychiatrists to be more conservative than PCPs in prescribing psychotropic medications in cases also amenable to verbal psychotherapy can also work against them. Since in the short run medication is often less expensive than psychotherapy, and given that the outcomes research indicates comparable efficacy, managed care companies promote the use of medications for common outpatient problems such as depression.[16]

In managed care environments, psychiatrists' talents are often being tapped only when the less expensive route has failed and when patients are suicidal, homicidal, self-injurious, psychotic, self-destructively substance abusive, and/or refractory to conventional medication. Nevertheless, studies are emerging that the utilization of psychiatrists from the outset of a treatment regimen has a significant positive effect on cost reduction and clinical outcome.

F.   Increased Use of Non-Physicians Instead of Psychiatrists

Under the old fee-for-service system, third-party payers attempted to control their costs in a number of ways. One way was to restrict patient access to specific clinicians. At one time health insurance coverage was only available for services provided by a physician. What limited mental health care plans covered had to be delivered by a psychiatrist. During the 1970s, this restriction was altered to allow care by a doctoral-level psychologist, as long as the patient was referred by a physician. Eventually, psychologists were recognized as independent clinicians by the third-party payers.

As managed care has evolved, this method to control costs has completely reversed. Many managed care organizations now seek out clinicians on the basis of their costs per session. Currently, most MCOs

---

[16] Chambliss, C. "Meeting the Challenges of Managed Mental Health Care." *Perspectives: A Mental Health Magazine*, 1996 © Mental Health Net & CMHC Systems.

are using psychologists, social workers, marriage and family therapists, nurse clinicians, and drug and alcohol counselors in addition to psychiatrists.

A 1996 survey by the American Association for Marriage and Family Therapy of the composition of 15 managed mental health care clinician panels found that physicians were in the minority. Figure 6 shows the number of companies surveyed whose networks are composed of the corresponding percentages of each discipline.

G.   Emphasis on Performance Indicators

In order to survive as a business in a very competitive market, managed care must document its performance for its clients. Patient satisfaction is one of the key performance indicators. A patient may receive the best of care but be dissatisfied for a variety of reasons such as poor telephone access, excessive waiting time in the clinician's office, or confusing or complex paperwork. If enough patients from a specific group voice dissatisfaction, the purchaser may consider changing managed care vendors.

Companies must also be able to demonstrate that their clinicians are providing effective care at the least cost. In order to do this they will continue to develop outcomes indicators to measure their clinicians' performance. They will have to be able to document their diagnostic decisions, treatment plans, and outcomes.

MCO Panel Makeup by Discipline

FIGURE 6

Percentage	M.D.	Ph.D.	Social Worker
30% or more	1	10	8*
20%–29%	6	2	4
10%–19%	6	1	1
Less than 10%	2	2	2

*Two of the eight reported that their networks were 50% and 70% M.S.W.s.

Source: Practice Strategies, 1996.

At the same time, psychiatrists' administrative support systems will also have to continue to improve in efficiency in order to keep overhead expenses under control and competitive. Psychiatrists must become familiar with the terms and concepts of the business culture where their role will be determined on the basis of cost-benefit analyses.

H.   Loss of Access to the Public Mental Health System by Employed Individuals

Medicaid has historically been a safety net for individuals with serious mental illnesses that required long-term treatment that was not covered under their employers' health plans. As the public mental health system adopts managed care concepts and practices, it will be forced to restrict certain social services it has traditionally provided to the seriously or chronically mentally ill. This will result in a loss of access to services that previously benefitted many employed mentally ill people.

A major unresolved question arising from the introduction of managed mental health care into the public system centers around these chronically mentally ill and disabled patients traditionally served by the public sector. How will they be "managed"? Can the cost of their care be incorporated into a capitated, risk-sharing program? If not, where will these individuals go for needed services?

I.   Psychiatrists' Roles in Public Managed Care Systems

The patients receiving care through a publicly funded delivery system comprise an extremely low-income and vulnerable population—one that is often unprepared to make informed choices based on their rights to be served by the public system and to receive the respect and access to quality care to which they are entitled. In short, psychiatrists need to be actively involved in the selections and ongoing monitoring of public managed care systems, with respect to a variety of issues, which are outlined below.

Patient rights In all public managed care delivery systems, psychiatrists' (and in fact all) patients should be guaranteed the right to:

- Receive easily understandable materials describing benefits and operational protocols, including provisions for patients who cannot read, at the time of enrollment and going forward, upon request;

- Be involved in all treatment decisions, including giving or withholding consent to receive services and amending their consent as the treatment plan is modified;

- Refuse any treatment without being disenrolled;

- Be assured that their privacy will be protected;

- Access their own records;

- Receive services without significant language or cultural barriers;

- Access a full array of treatment alternatives to prevent the need for involuntary commitment;

- File grievances and provide feedback about their satisfaction with services; and

- Appeal any decisions about their care.

Psychiatrists should also advocate for public managed care systems to operate under a "no eject/no reject" philosophy concerning enrollment in the program. Disenrollment should not be allowed on the basis of pre-existing conditions, diagnosis, high treatment expenses, missed appointments, refusal of treatment, or failure to complete required paperwork. There must also be appropriate appeals and due process mechanisms in place for patients who are disenrolled and for psychiatrists to advocate for their patients directly.

Triage The psychiatrist (and any other clinician) functioning as the triage clinician is responsible for assessing the patient's functioning with respect to living situation, work, school, family, peer group, and community, in addition to his or her mental and physical health.

Psychiatrists should ensure that any public managed care systems they participate in develop, monitor, and report their performance on access standards, including, but not limited to:

- Appointment waiting times;

- Availability of evening and weekend hours;

- Geographic convenience;

- Availability of public transportation; and

- Handicap accessibility.

Additionally, there should be no financial or other incentives prohibiting or hindering access to care, nor should there be gatekeepers limiting access to psychiatrists or other specialists.

Clinicians, programs, and facilities Based on the information obtained during the assessment, the psychiatrist makes a determination about the appropriate type of service(s) for the patient. In a population as diverse as that found in the public sector, it is critical that a full and coordinated continuum of service options be available. Although some locations may have limited services and clinicians, public managed care systems should provide access to an extensive array of services, including, but not limited to:

- Acute inpatient care;

- Partial hospitalization/day treatment;

- Residential treatment;

- Outpatient services;

- School-based services;

- Home-based services;

- Respite care;

- Psychiatric rehabilitation;

- Detoxification;

- 24-hour crisis intervention;

- Crisis/observation beds;

- Outpatient crisis stabilization;

- Medication management;

- Case management;

- Assertive outreach for the homeless;

- Self-help groups;

- Rent-subsidized, independent living;

- Intensive home-based services;

- Independent living support services;

- Therapeutic foster care;

- Therapeutic and group homes;

- Screening and prevention;

- Family support and education;

- Family therapy;

- Occupational therapy;

- Court-ordered treatment; and

- Psychiatric consultation-liaison services.

Psychiatrists will often be responsible for coordinating various patient services and should play an active role in the full spectrum of clinical specialists working to meet patient needs (often as team leader, team participant, or consultant to a treatment team). A comprehensive network will facilitate the establishment of multi-disciplinary approaches, which are often in the best interest of patients in the public system.

Benefits Psychiatrists should ensure that program benefits are not contradictory to providing services that meet accepted medical standards, including, but not limited to, the practice guidelines developed by the American Psychiatric Association. Psychiatrists should also ensure that appropriate and separate benefits are available for high utilizers, such as people with serious and/or chronic mental illness, who are likely to be under their care. Criteria for such benefits should be based on chronic and persistent functional impairment and risk factors, independent of diagnosis. The benefits should include long-term care management, rehabilitative services, access to affordable housing, continuous clinical follow-up, and intermittent acute treatment at times of crisis.

Prevention and outreach Prevention and outreach services are extremely important in meeting the mental health needs of public sector populations. In the public sector, these services encompass very different activities from prevention and outreach in the private sector. Because of this, managed care companies that have traditionally operated in the private, employer sector have little experience in developing such programs for public sector patients. Thus, psychiatrists must work with their state agencies to ensure that these services are provided appropriately by the managed care entity administering the program.

The most effective way of accomplishing this is by addressing these issues during the RFP process and ensuring that information on how these services will be provided is included in the program contract. In addition, psychiatrists working in these systems will need to develop an awareness of available programs, such as parenting education, training for at-risk mothers and substance-abusing mothers, clubhouses, etc. It is also important for psychiatrists to develop linkages with primary care and other available mental health services as part of the prevention mechanism.

Cultural competence Psychiatrists and other clinicians providing care in public systems must be culturally competent. As defined by Cross et al. (1989), cultural competence is "a set of congruent behaviors, attitudes, and policies that come together in a system, agency, or among professionals which enables the system, agency, or professionals to work effectively in cross-cultural situations." While related to the more commonly used concepts of cultural awareness, sensitivity, and appropriateness, cultural competence is much more than any of these concepts. It moves beyond knowledge gained about any particular group through reading, studies, or experiential exposure to a minority group other than one's own, to focus on building a system that includes four essential elements: valuing diversity, awareness of the "dynamics of difference," ability to institutionalize cultural knowledge, and cultural self-assessment.

The following are some basic principles of cultural competence of which psychiatrists should be aware:

- Behavior and attitude change must start at the top; cultural knowledge must be incorporated into the policy-making process as well as the clinical care system.

- The system, and the psychiatrist practicing within it, must recognize that minority populations are at the very least bicultural, and in some cases multi-cultural, and that this status creates a unique set of mental health issues to which the system must be equipped to respond.

- Individuals and families make treatment choices based on cultural forces, which must be considered if the treatment provided by the psychiatrists is to be effective.

- Inherent in cross-cultural interactions are dynamics that must be acknowledged, adjusted to, and accepted. Cultural competence for psychiatrists involves working in conjunction with natural, informal support and helping networks within the minority community.

- Cultural competence is achieved through committed personal and institutional leadership at all levels of the program. Psychiatrists should insist on nothing less.

- Cultural competence requires demonstrated respect for and sensitivity to cultural differences by all involved parties, including the psychiatrist.

- Cultural competence requires the integration of culturally competent principles, beliefs, behaviors, and attitudes throughout all levels of the system.

- Cultural competence goes beyond linguistic competence and requires integration of cultural norms into treatment setting and practices, including knowledge of culturally accepted healing practices and collaboration with culturally accepted healers.

- Cultural competence requires the development of quality indicators and quantitative measures appropriate to each culture.

- Cultural competence requires that psychiatrists pay attention to the retention and development of culturally diverse staff, not just to their recruitment and hiring.

Information management To ensure coordination of care and reduce the duplication of services, a single record in the information system should follow the patient as he or she moves through the care delivery system. Information concerning dates of service, type of service, and outcomes should be contained in the record, and all agencies and clinicians delivering treatment and related services, including psychiatrists, should document their activities in this record. As part of the program design, public managed care systems should develop and implement policies concerning the frequency and level of detail required in such documentation. Psychiatrists should have direct input into this process.

Psychiatrists and others involved in clinical treatment and administration must ensure that patient-specific information entered into the system remains confidential. Information management systems should adhere to the Joint Commission on Accreditation of Healthcare Organization's (JCAHO's) standards for information systems, medical records, and patient confidentiality. There should also be policies regarding how patient confidentiality is to be preserved, with special attention to obtaining consent, incorporating passwords and other data security measures, and complying with any state laws concerning confidentiality. Psychiatrists active in public systems should ensure that such policies comply with medical standards.

Final Thoughts Related to the Psychiatrist's Roles in Public Systems

- Psychiatrists should not be denied an advocacy role on behalf of their patients.

- The standard clinical professional contract should be made public.

- Psychiatrists should have access to clinical criteria and protocols and procedures.

- Psychiatrists should have an opportunity to discuss and negotiate their roles in mental health care delivery systems and linkages to primary care.

Most importantly, psychiatrists, patients, their families, and other stakeholders should be involved in the development and ongoing monitoring of public mental health systems—in all environments, including managed care. We strongly encourage APA members who are having difficulty with issues related to managed care and public systems to contact the Office of Economic Affairs and Practice Management at 202-682-6212.

This monograph has examined the evolution of public mental health in the United States and has explored eligibility requirements and payment mechanisms within the Medicaid programs. A significant number of states have applied for—and received—waivers from HCFA, thereby allowing the implementation of managed care models to the delivery of health care services in the public sector. Managed care models, particularly in the form of HMOs, have begun to be applied to the Medicare sector as well. These managed care paradigms will affect the mechanisms by which patients access public sector psychiatric care, how psychotropic medications are financed, and the manner in which care is provided for those with serious mental illness and children with serious emotional disturbances.

VII

Psychiatrists practicing within the public sector will feel the repercussions of the initiation and propagation of managed care. The degree to which these professionals confront—and ultimately adapt—to this evolving landscape will undoubtedly be the subject of intense scrutiny and debate in the years to come.

APA Resources and Services for Psychiatrists

Psychiatrists in need of more information or help with public system and other professional issues can contact numerous American Psychiatric Association (APA) resources.

APA's Consultation Service—202-682-6203

APA's Legal Consultation Plan—202-682-6064

APA's Managed Care Help Line—800-343-4671

APA's Office of Economic Affairs and Practice Management—
202-682-6212

The APA's address is 1400 K Street, NW, Washington, D.C. 20005.

Public Mental Health Bibliography

American Academy of Child and Adolescent Psychiatry (1996) *Best Principles for Managed Care Medicaid RFPs: How Decision-Makers Can Select and Monitor High Quality Programs.* Washington, D.C.

American Managed Behavioral Healthcare Association and National Association of State Mental Health Program Directors (1997) *White paper in progress, Public Mental Health Systems: Medicaid Re-structuring and Managed Behavioral Healthcare.* Washington, D.C.: American Managed Behavioral Healthcare Association.

Branch, C. (1995) *Designing Capitation Projects for Persons With Severe Mental Illness: A Policy Guide for State and Local Officials.* Boston, MA: Technical Assistance Collaborative.

Chambliss, C. (1996) Meeting the challenges of managed mental health care. *Perspectives: A Mental Health Magazine,* Volume 1, Number 5.

Commonwealth of Pennsylvania, Department of Public Welfare (1996) HealthChoices '96. Request for Proposals.

Coughlin, K. (Ed.) (1996) Concept paper: Mental health and substance abuse managed care, *1997 Behavioral Managed Care Sourcebook.* New York, NY: Faulkner and Gray.

Cross, T.L., Bazron, B.J. & Dennis, K.W., et al. (1989) *Toward a Culturally Competent System of Care.* Washington, D.C.: Georgetown University Child Development Center.

England, M. & Cole, R. (1993) Children and mental health: How can the system be improved? *Health Affairs,* Volume 14, Number 3.

IX

Health Care Financing Administration, Medicaid Bureau (FY 1994–1995) *Form HCFA-64.* Washington, D.C.

Iowa Medicaid Managed Mental Health Care Plan (1995) Contract Between State of Iowa, Department of Human Services, and Medco Behavioral Care Corporation of Iowa.

Koyanagi, C. (1996) *Managing Managed Care for Publicly Financed Mental Health Services.* Washington, D.C.: Bazelon Center for Mental Health Law.

Mechanic, D. & Aiken, L. (1989) *Capitation in Mental Health: Promises and Pitfalls of Capitation* (New Directions for Mental Health Services.) San Francisco, CA: Jossey-Bass.

National Alliance for the Mentally Ill (1995) *Mental Illness and Managed Care: A Primer for Families and Consumers.* Washington, D.C.

National Resource Network for Child and Family Mental Health Services (1997) *The Role of the Child and Adolescent Psychiatrist in Multi-agency Systems of Care.* San Francisco, CA: American Jewish Press Association.

Oss, M.E. (Ed.) (1991) Industry statistics: CMHC private sector funding declines while care for seriously mentally ill remains high. *OPEN MINDS,* Volume 4, Number 5.

Oss, M.E. (1991) Non-psychiatric physicians prescribe more tranquilizers than psychiatrists. *OPEN MINDS,* Volume 4, Issue 8.

Oss, M.E. & Mackie, J.J. (1995) Behavioral health finance: How did we get here? *OPEN MINDS,* Volume 9, Issue 7.

Oss, M.E. & Moghul, A. (1996) The managed behavioral health care industry: Overview and future prospects, *1997 Behavioral Managed Care Sourcebook.* New York, NY: Faulkner and Gray.

Powell, C.K. & Straub, J.H. (1996) *Medicare Managed Care Manual.* New York, NY: Thompson Publishing Group.

Ray, C.G. & Oss, M.E. (1993) National community mental healthcare council. *OPEN MINDS,* Volume 6, Issue 2.

Sack, L. & Seiverts, S. (1988) Pro & con: Should psychoanalysis be covered in health benefit plans? *OPEN MINDS,* Volume 1, Number 9.

Schaffer, I. & Frederick, L. (1995) What are the implications of universal rates for psychotherapy? *Behavioral Health Practice Advisor,* Volume 1, Number 10.

IX

Sipkoff, M.E. & Oss, M.E. (1995) How to avoid strategic planning pitfalls. *OPEN MINDS,* Volume 8, Issue 11.

Starr, P. (1982). *The Social Transformation of American Medicine.* New York, NY: Basic Books, Inc.

State Mental Health Representatives for Children and Youth Division of the National Association of State Mental Health Program Directors (1995) *Successful Integration of System of Care Development With Managed Behavioral Healthcare Technologies in Public Children's Mental Health.* Alexandria, VA: National Association of State Mental Health Program Directors.

Tuttle, G. (1996) MCOs report lower fees, broader services. *Practice Strategies,* Volume 2, Issue 8, Washington, D.C.: American Association for Marriage and Family Therapy.

Urban Institute, The (1996) *HCFA 64 and HCFA 2082 reports.* Washington, D.C.

U.S. Department of Health and Human Services, Office of National Health Statistics, Office of the Actuary (1997) Washington, D.C.

U.S. Department of Health and Human Services news release (June 14, 1996). Http://www.acf.dhhs.gov/ACFNews/news/welfref.html.

Warren, R.V. (1995) *Social Work Practice Update: Merging Managed Care and Medicaid: Private Regulation of Public Health Care.* Washington, D.C.: National Association of Social Workers.

Yennie, H. & Oss, M.E. (1997) New York City SMI/SNP rates: Between $10K and $12K. *OPEN MINDS,* Volume 11, Issue 1.

Public Mental Health Glossary

Accessibility Degree to which the health care delivery system inhibits or facilitates the ability of an individual to gain entry and to receive services (includes geographic, transportation, social, time, and financial considerations).

Administrative Services Only (ASO) Plan An arrangement under which an insurance carrier or an independent organization will, for a fee, handle the administration of claims, benefits, and other administrative functions for a self-insured group.

Allowable Costs Charges for services rendered or supplies furnished by a psychiatrist or other clinician which qualify as covered expenses.

Alternative Care Medical care received in lieu of inpatient hospitalization. Examples include partial hospital, residential treatment, and structured outpatient programs.

Alternative Delivery System (ADS) A method of providing health care benefits that departs from traditional indemnity methods. An HMO, for example, can be said to be an alternative delivery system.

APA American Psychiatric Association.

Average Length of Stay (ALOS) Average number of patient days of service rendered to each inpatient (excluding newborns) during a given period. Varies for patients by diagnosis, age, hospital efficiency, etc. One measure of use of health facilities.

Balance Billing A clinician's billing of a covered person for charges above the amount reimbursed by the health plan (i.e., the difference between billed charges and the amount paid). This may or may not be appropriate, depending upon the contractual arrangements between the parties.

Base Capitation A stipulated dollar amount to cover the cost of health care per covered person, less mental health/substance abuse services, pharmacy and administrative charges.

Basic Health Services Benefits that all federally qualified HMOs must offer, defined under Subpart A, 110.102 of the federal HMO Regulations.

Beneficiary The person designated or provided for by the policy terms to receive benefits under the insurance contract.

Capitation A stipulated dollar amount established to cover the cost of health care services delivered for a person. The term

X

usually refers to a negotiated per capita rate to be paid periodically, usually monthly, for the delivery of all health service required by the covered person under the condition of the clinician contract. The payment is the same regardless of the amount of services rendered.

Carve-out A separate financing and delivery structure established for a particular group of benefits typically provided by an indemnity or HMO plan. Example: A mental health benefit may be carved out, and a specialized vendor selected to supply these services on a stand-alone basis. These arrangements are usually provided for a fixed fee per subscriber or per member per month. Also sometimes referred to as single service plans (SSP). See also Capitation.

Case Management A process whereby beneficiaries with specific health care needs are identified and a plan is developed which uses health care resources to achieve the optimum patient outcome in the most efficient, cost-effective manner. It typically involves parties—the payer, the clinician, the patient, and the family—in an effort to find the most appropriate treatment for the patient.

Claim A demand to the insurer for the payments of benefits under an insurance contract.

Community Health Management Information System (CHMIS) A system to electronically link clinicians, payers, employers, and patients in communities to improve health care quality and promote community wellness.

Community Mental Health Centers (CMHCs) Centers designed to provide comprehensive, integrated, and coordinated systems of mental health and substance abuse care in the least restrictive environment. Such centers were created as a result of federal legislation in the mid-1960s.

Concurrent Review A routine review of the medical necessity for continued treatment, by an internal or external utilization reviewer, during the course of a patient's treatment. This usually occurs for inpatient, residential, and partial hospitalization treatment, though it is becoming more common for outpatient treatment as well.

Continuum of Care A range of clinical services provided to an individual or group which may reflect treatment rendered during a single patient hospitalization or may include care for multiple conditions during a lifetime. The continuum provides a basis for analyzing quality, cost, and utilization in the long term.

Cost-Shifting The practice by some clinicians of redistributing the difference between normal charges and amounts received from certain payers by increasing charges made to other payers.

Credentialing A process of review to approve a clinician who applies to participate in a health plan. Specific criteria and prerequisites are applied in determining initial and ongoing participation in the health plan.

Cultural Competency The understanding of the social, linguistic, ethnic, and behavioral characteristics of a community or population and the ability to translate that knowledge systematically into practices in the delivery of mental health services. Such understanding may be reflected, for example, in the ability to identify and value differences, acknowledge the interactive dynamics of cultural differences, continually expand cultural knowledge and resources with regard to populations served, commit to cross-cultural training of staff, and develop policies to provide relevant, effective programs for the diversity of people served.

Deductible Annual expenses a subscriber must pay before an insurance plan covers health care costs. These often apply to a subscriber and his or her family in total.

Drug Formulary A listing of prescription medications which are preferred for use by the health plan and which will be dispensed through participating pharmacies to covered individuals. This list is subject to periodic review and modification by the health plan. A plan that has adopted an open or voluntary formulary allows coverage for both formulary and nonformulary medications. A plan that has adopted a closed, select, or mandatory formulary limits coverage to those drugs in the formulary.

Dual Eligibility A description of beneficiaries who are eligible to receive benefits under both the Medicaid and Medicare systems.

Employee Retirement Income Security Act of 1974, Public Law 93-406 (ERISA) This law mandates reporting and disclosure requirements for group life and health plans.

Exclusions Charges, services, or supplies that are not covered by a health insurance plan.

Exclusive Provider Organization (EPO) A managed care organization designates a single clinician where services may be rendered. The term is derived from the term preferred provider organization (PPO). However, where a PPO generally extends coverage for non-preferred provider services as well as preferred provider services, an EPO provides coverage only for contracted clinicians. Technically,

many HMOs also can be described at EPOs.

Fee Maximum The maximum amount a participating provider may be paid for a specific health care service provided to plan members under a specific contract. A comprehensive listing of fee maximums used to reimburse physicians and/or other clinicians on a fee-for-service basis is called a fee schedule.

Fee-for-Service A traditional means of billing by health clinicians for each service performed, referring to payment in specific amounts for specific services rendered (as opposed to a retainer, salary, or other contract arrangements). In relation to the patient, it refers to payment in specific amounts for specific services rendered.

Fee Schedule A listing of fees or allowances for specific medical procedures, which usually represents the maximum amounts the program will pay for specific procedures.

Flat Schedule A type of benefits schedule in group insurance under which everyone is insured for the same benefits, regardless of salary, position, or other circumstances.

Gatekeeper A primary care physician who serves as the patient's initial contact for medical care and who makes referrals. The gatekeeper's function is to reduce health care utilization and costs.

Guidelines Systematically developed statements on medical practice that assist psychiatrists and patients in making decisions about appropriate health care for specific medical conditions. Guidelines are frequently used to evaluate appropriateness and medical necessity of care. Terms used synonymously include practice parameters, standard treatment protocols, and clinical practice guidelines.

X

Outcomes can be used as information to modify or improve guidelines.

Health Maintenance Organization (HMO) An organization that provides comprehensive medical care for a fixed annual fee. Physicians and other health professionals often are on salary or on contract with the HMO to provide services. Patients are assigned a primary care physician or nurse as a gatekeeper, who decides what health services are needed and when.

Health Plan Employer Data and Information Set (HEDIS) A core set of performance measures to assist employers and other health purchasers in understanding the value of health care purchases and evaluating health plan performance. Developed by the National Committee for Quality Assurance.

Indemnity An insurance program in which the insured person is reimbursed for covered expenses. It is a traditional health insurance plan with little or no benefit management, a fee-for-service reimbursement model, and few, if any, restrictions on clinician selections.

Individual Practice Association (IPA) A health care model that contracts with an entity, which in turn contracts with physicians, to provide health care services in return for a negotiated fee. Physicians continue in their existing individual or group practices and are compensated on a per capita, fee schedule, or fee-for-service basis.

Integrated Delivery System A generic term referring to a combination of clinicians to deliver health care in an integrated way. Some models of integration include physician hospital organizations, a management services organization, group practice without walls, integrated

clinician organization, and medical foundation.

Length of Stay (LOS) The number of days that a covered person stayed in an inpatient facility.

Managed Behavioral Health Organization (MBHO) An organization that assumes responsibility for managing the mental health benefit for an employer or payer organization. The management may range from utilization management services to the actual provision of the services through its own staff network. Reimbursement may be on a fee-for-service, shared risk, or full-risk capitated basis.

Managed Care A system that manages or controls what health care spends by closely monitoring how physicians and other medical professionals treat patients. Various techniques for keeping costs down include limiting coverage to care provided by specially selected doctors and hospitals and requiring preauthorization for hospital care and other services.

Management Services Organization (MSO) A legal entity that provides practice management, administrative and support services to individual physicians or group practices. An MSO may be a direct subsidiary of a hospital or may be owned by investors.

Medicaid A program, adopted in 1965, of health insurance for eligible disabled and low-income people, administered by the federal government and participating states. The program's costs are shared by the federal and state governments and are paid for by general tax revenue.

Medicare A nationwide, federally administered health insurance program which covers the costs of hospitalization, medical care, and some related services

X

for eligible people. Medicare has two parts: Part A covers inpatient costs, and Part B covers outpatient and physician costs.

Medicare Supplement Policy A policy guaranteeing that a health plan will pay a policyholder's coinsurance, deductibles, and copayments and may provide additional health plan or non-Medicare coverage for services up to a predefined benefit limit. In essence, the policy pays for the portion of the cost of services not covered by Medicare. Also called Medigap or Medicare wrap.

Patient Days Accumulated total, for the reporting period, of the number of patients in a hospital each day (excluding newborns). A patient day is one patient in one hospital bed for one day.

Peer Review Organization (PRO) An entity established by the Tax Equity and Fiscal Responsibility Act of 1982 (TEFRA) to review quality of care and appropriateness of admissions, readmissions, and discharges for Medicare and Medicaid. These organizations are held responsible for maintaining and lowering admission rates and reducing lengths of stay while ensuring against inadequate treatment. Also known as professional standards review organization (PSRO).

Per Diem An agreed upon rate per inpatient, residential, or partial hospitalization day that is all-inclusive. All ancillary services, in addition to therapies and room and board, are included in this rate. Sometimes the psychiatrists' services are included, and in these situations, the per diem is referred to as global.

Physician-Hospital Organization (PHO) A legal entity formed and owned by one or more hospital and physician groups to obtain payer contracts and to further mutual interests. Physicians maintain ownership of their practices while agreeing to accept managed care patients under the terms of the PHO agreement. The PHO serves as a negotiating, contacting, and marketing unit.

Point-of-Service (POS) A provision that allows patients in managed-care plans which limit choice of physicians and hospitals to seek treatment outside of the plans. Patients who use this option typically are required to pay more.

Preferred Provider Organization (PPO) A variation of the traditional fee-for-service care arrangement representing a group of physicians, dentists, and/or hospitals and other clinicians that contracts with employers, unions, or third-party administrators to provide beneficiaries with services at competitive rates. Beneficiaries have free choice among the physicians in a PPO arrangement. The beneficiary is not penalized or prevented from using his or her regular physician, even if that physician does not participate in the PPO. PPOs usually provide incentives for participation, such as a competitive rate structure. In addition, PPOs generally use primary care physicians to ensure that hospitalization occurs only when absolutely necessary, with extensive concurrent utilization review.

Primary Care Medical practice based on direct contact with the patient without referral from another physician. Such practice is undertaken by physicians in various ways including pediatricians, obstetricians, internists, family physicians, and general clinicians. In addition, many specialists engage in a significant amount of primary care.

Primary Care Network (PCN) A group of primary care physicians who have

X

joined together to share the risk of providing care to their patients who are covered by a given health plan.

Primary Care Physician (PCP) A physician the majority of whose practice is devoted to internal medicine, family/general practice, and/or pediatrics.

Primary Data Information obtained from medical records or other primary sources of clinical findings, such as diagnostic tests and physical examination results.

Referral Clinician A clinician (usually a specialty physician or other health entity) who renders a service to a patient who has been referred to him/her by a participating clinician in the health plan.

Resource-Based Relative Value Scale (RBRVS) A fee schedule introduced by HCFA to reimburse physicians' Medicare fees based on the amount of time, resources, and expertise expended in selected specific medical procedures. Adjustments are made for regional variations in rents, wages, and other geographical differences.

Retrospective Review Determination of medical necessity and/or appropriate billing practice for services already rendered.

RFP Request for proposals.

Risk The chance or possibility of loss. In insurance terms, it is the probability of financial loss associated with a given population. The term may also be applied to physicians, who may be held at risk if hospitalization rates exceed agreed-upon thresholds. The sharing of risk is often employed as a utilization control mechanism within the managed care setting.

Risk Analysis The process of evaluating expected medical care costs for a prospective group and determining what product, benefit level, and price to offer in order to bear an acceptable amount of risk.

Risk-Sharing A method by which premiums and costs of medical protection are shared by plan sponsors, participants, and clinicians.

Substance Abuse and Mental Health Services Administration (SAMHSA) A division under the Department of Health and Human Services charged with collecting managed care data and assisting states and municipalities with quality improvement and program monitoring. The division assists patients in the establishment of relationships with organizations that are providing mental health care.

Third-Party Administrator (TPA) An independent person or corporate entity (third party) that administers group benefits and claims for a self-insured company or group. A TPA does not underwrite the risk.

Third-Party Payer The insurer who pays for the services provided to a patient.

Utilization The extent to which the members of a covered group use a program or obtain a particular service, or category of services, during a given period of time. Usually expressed as the number of services used per year or per 100 or 1,000 people eligible for the service.

Utilization Management The close management of patient utilization of health care services inside a managed health care program.

Utilization Review (UR) A formal assessment of the medical necessity, efficiency, and/or appropriateness of health care services and treatment plans on a prospective, concurrent, or retrospective basis.

X

Waiver A request to HCFA to forgo certain federal Medicaid requirements. This has been a mechanism for states to implement managed care financing models to a portion of the public mental health system. Two waivers have particular significance, Section 1915(b) and Section 1115 waivers, which differ in the degree of restructuring allowed by the states within the Medicaid program.